Your Five Senses and Your Sixth Sense

Touch

Connor Dayton

PowerKiDS press
New York

Published in 2014 by The Rosen Publishing Group, Inc.
29 East 21st Street, New York, NY 10010

First Edition

Editor: Jennifer Way
Book Design: Kate Vlachos

Photo Credits: Cover AlikeYou/Shutterstock.com; pp. 4, 24 (skin) Joy Brown/Shutterstock.com; p. 7 Huw Jones/Lonely Planet Images/Getty Images; pp. 8, 24 (fingertips) Jeffrey Hamilton/Lifesize/Getty Images; p. 11 Jose Luis Pelaez/Iconica/Getty Images; p. 12 Scholastic Studio 10/Photolibrary/Getty Images; p. 15 © iStockphoto.com/Elna Elisseeva; p. 16 BSIP/UIG/ Universal Images Group/Getty Images; p. 19 spectrumblue/Shutterstock.com; p. 20 3445128471/Shutterstock.com; p. 23 Syda Productions/Shutterstock.com; p. 24 (braille) © iStockphoto.com/chatsimo; p. 24 (nerves) ducu59us/Shutterstock.com.

Library of Congress Cataloging-in-Publication Data

Dayton, Connor, author.
  Touch / by Connor Dayton. — First edition.
      pages cm. — (Your senses)
  Includes bibliographical references and index.
  ISBN 978-1-4777-2855-0 (library binding) — ISBN 978-1-4777-2948-9 (pbk.) —
ISBN 978-1-4777-3025-6 (6-pack)
  1. Touch—Juvenile literature. I. Title.
  QP451.D36 2014
  612.8'8—dc23
                          2013016397

Manufactured in the United States of America

CPSIA Compliance Information: Batch #W14PK3: For Further Information contact Rosen Publishing, New York, New York at 1-800-237-9932

CONTENTS

4

Touch is one of your five senses. Your **skin** senses touch. Skin is your largest organ!

Your skin has three layers. It is extra thick on your palms.

7

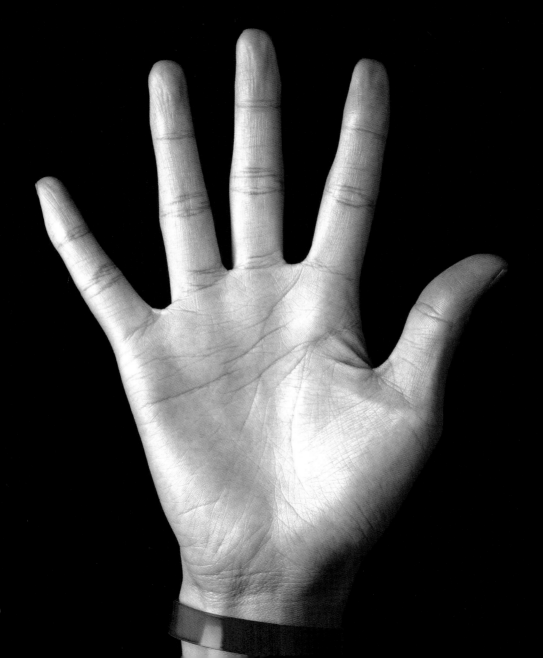

8

Fingertips are sensitive. They sense touch well. The middle of the back is the least sensitive body part.

Your skin has **nerves**. Nerves pick up signals when you touch things.

Nerves send signals to your brain. Your brain tells you what you touch.

Touch can tell you if
something is wet.

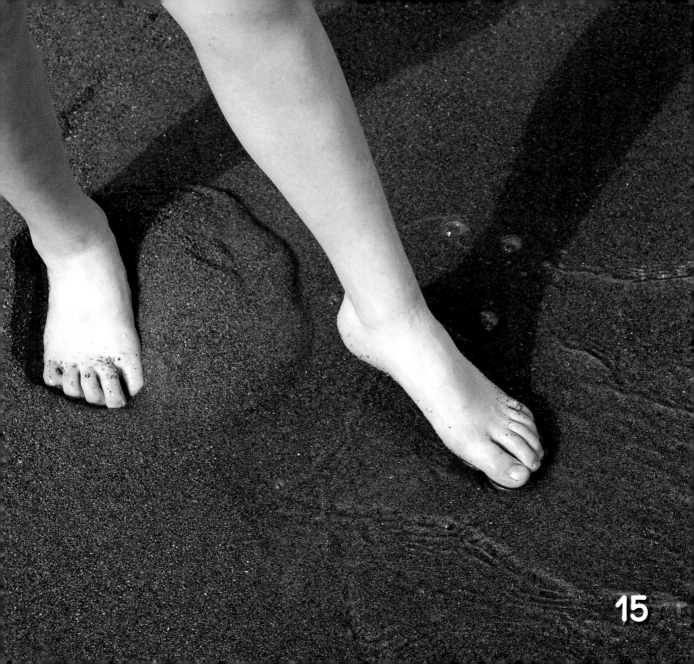

15

People who are blind read using touch. They read **Braille** with their fingers.

Some things you touch are sharp. Some are soft.

Some things are too hot to touch. They will burn you. Third degree burns are the worst kind.

You use your sense of touch all the time. What have you touched today?

WORDS TO KNOW

Braille

fingertips

nerve

skin

INDEX

WEBSITES

Due to the changing nature of Internet links, PowerKids Press has developed an online list of websites related to the subject of this book. This site is updated regularly. Please use this link to access the list:
www.powerkidslinks.com/yfsyss/touch/